THE DYNAMICS OF FAITH

David Ade Olushola

The Dynamics of Faith
ISBN: 978-87-970442-2-3

Contact: adeolushola@gmail.com

Printed in Denmark

CONTENTS

INTRODUCTION

The evidence of a progressive and dynamic faith is found in the letter of Apostle Paul to the Thessalonians;

2 Thessalonians 1:3 We are bound to thank God always for you, brethren, as it is meet, because that your faith groweth exceedingly, and the charity of every one of you all toward each other aboundeth;

Paul says firstly in the above passage that it was necessary for him to be thankful to God because the faith of the people is growing exceedingly and as it happens everywhere with the subject matter, so also in this Church. Their growing faith is changing the attitude and actions of the brethren for better. Notice that as their faith grew, so did their love and care for one another.
The results of a growing faith are visible, and the effect of such is first evident in the immediate environment.

This great gift from God to humanity is crucial to man's existence and purpose on planet earth. One cannot please God without it.

Exercising faith in God's grace is the way to live. Faith in the gospel releases God's power to assist us to do what ordinary man cannot do. Let me mention some of the things faith allows us to do.

It is through faith in God's grace that one is first SAVED

and not by works Ephesians 2:8

Every believer is charged to LIVE by it Habakkuk 2:4, Rom 1:17, Gal 3.11, Heb 10:38

We are again admonished to WALK by it and not by sight 2 Corinthians 5:7

It is the ONLY FIGHT a believer is encouraged to fight 1 Timothy 6:12

It is the believer's VICTORY that overcomes the world 1 John 5:4

It is the Christian's ARMOR that quenches the fiery darts of the enemy Ephesians 6:16

It provides a plausible way to PLEASE God Hebrews 11:6

This book AIMS to identify critical forces that can help make our faith come alive and be effective.
I aim to answer questions like;

How do I maximize my faith? How do I grow in faith?

What are the forces determining the outcome of my faith?

THE DOMINION OF MAN

God has not only given you dominion over your life (the power and the authority to govern and control), but He has also commissioned you to subdue (to bring low and utterly defeat) those things that are not in agreement with His will for your life (Genesis 1:26-28).

God made us in His 'image' and 'likeness' (just like Him), and He gave us the same ability to rule by using the most powerful force in the universe: FAITH! (The absolute trust and confidence in God's Word.) God believes his word, and He will have you do the same.

According to Genesis, God made the earth and the fullness thereof, giving Adam dominion over all the works of His hands. In other words, Adam was the god of this world. God entrusted the planet earth into the hand of man. He made man to be the caretaker thereof. God's original intent is that man should rule the earth, and He has not changed his mind about that.

Genesis 1:26 And God said, Let us make man in our image, after our likeness: and let them have dominion over the fish of the sea, and over the fowl of the air, and over the cattle, and over all the earth, and over every creeping thing that creepeth upon the earth.

27 So God created man in his own image, in the image of God created he him; male and female created he them.

28 And God blessed them, and God said unto them, <u>Be fruitful, and multiply, and replenish the earth, and subdue it: and have dominion</u> over the fish of the sea, and over the fowl of the air, and over every living thingthat moveth upon the earth.

So we read that man was created in God's image and basically after His likeness and man was given a domain of influence which is the earth to exercise his authority. We are not to have dominion over other human beings but over our circumstances.

The book of Psalms affirmed this;

Psalms 115:16 The heaven, even the heavens, are the Lord's: but the earth hath he given to the children ofmen.

Psalms 8:6 Thou madest him (Man) to have dominion over the works of thy hands; thou hast put all thingsunder his feet:

So without any controversy, God placed Adam in charge of the planet. Adam, however, by his disobedience sold out to Satan, and Satan, through Adam, became the god of this world (2 Corinthians 4:4).
Satan then ruled over man until salvation came to man through Jesus Christ.
So we should examine man's situation after the fall of Adam, did man regain his authority or dominion?

Ephesians 2:1 Wherein <u>in time past</u> ye walked accor- ding to the course of this world, according to the prince of the power of the air, the spirit that now worketh in the children of disobedience:
3 Among whom also we all had our conversation in times past in the lusts of our fiesh, fulfilling the desires of the fiesh and of the mind; and were by nature the children of wrath, even as others.

Thanks to God through our Lord Jesus Christ for re-demption and restoration;

Ephesians 1:7 In whom we have redemption through his blood, the forgiveness of sins, according to the riches of his grace;

Colossians 1:12 Giving thanks unto the Father, which hath made us meet to be partakers of the inheritance of the saints in light:
13 Who hath <u>delivered us from the power of darkness, and hath translated us into the kingdom of his dearSon</u>:

Ephesians 2:4 But God, who is rich in mercy, for his great love wherewith he loved us,
5 Even when we were dead in sins, <u>hath quickenedus together with Christ</u>, (by grace ye are saved;)
6 And <u>hath raised us up together</u>, and <u>made us sittogether</u> in heavenly places in Christ Jesus:

Born again Christians are redeemed, translated, quickened, raised up and restored, sitting in the heavenly places in Christ Jesus far above all other powers. We are no longer slaves to Satan nor are we at his mercy but we have been integrated into the body of Christ and now are we far above all principality, power, might, and dominion;

Ephesians 1:18 The eyes of your understanding being enlightened; that ye may know what is the hope of his calling, and what the riches of the glory of his inheritance in the saints,

19   And what is the exceeding greatness of his power to us-ward who believe, according to the working ofhis mighty power,
20   Which he wrought in Christ, when he raised himfrom the dead, and set him at his own right hand in the heavenly places,
21   Far above all principality, and power, and might, and dominion, and every name that is named, not only in this world, but also in that which is to come: 22 And hath put all things under his feet, and gave him to be the head over all things to the church,
23 Which is his body, the fulness of him that filleth all in all.

This is why Satan has no right to rule us or dominate us anymore. The exceeding greatness of God's power to us-ward who believe is that our story has changed (Ephesians 2:1, 4-6). We have been raised up together with Christ, translated into the kingdom of light and power. We are joint heirs with Christ. We have authority over satanic forces through our Lord Jesus. But as it were, the average Christian has more faith in Satan's authority and power than in God's.

God's wisdom through the death and resurrection of Jesus Christ is to redeem man from the fall in Eden and restore the authority of man once again through Christ.

1 Corinthians 2.7 But we speak the wisdom of God in a mystery, even the hidden wisdom, which God ordained before the world unto our glory:
8 Which none of the princes of this world knew: for had they known it, they would not have crucified the Lord of glory.

The resurrection announced the defeat of God's adversary. The cross was the end game for the devil who has been fighting to destroy and overthrow the kingdom of God. Satan and his army did not see God's strategic victory plan otherwise they would not have crucified Jesus.

The resurrection secured our victory over sin and death. The Cross was heaven's triumph. And when Jesus Christ arose, the power of sin and death was broken. Thanks to God for the wisdom of the cross and the resurrection of our Lord Jesus Christ, for now, Christians need never fear Satan or death again.

Colossians 2:15 And having spoiled principalities and powers, he made a shew of them openly, triumphing over them in it.

Power has changed hands! Christ stripped Satan and all his demons of any power or authority they once had.

Believers only need enforce this victory. The curse of sin is broken, and death has lost its victory. He restored man back to God in His kingdom. Note that it is written that we are more than conquerors; Who is more than a conqueror but he who enjoys the spoil of VICTORY without ever participating in the battle.

Romans 8:37 Nay, in all these things we are more than conquerors through him that loved us.

Christ is the victor. The dominion Adam once lost, he regained back for man. The Church has been given the keys of the **"kingdom of heaven"** (Mathew 16:18-19). In the Holy Scripture and Jewish teaching, the handing over of keys implies promotion to full authority. Consider the following scriptures;

Mathew 28:18-19 And Jesus came and spake unto them, saying, All power is given unto me in heaven and in earth. Go ye therefore,...

Luke 10:19 Behold, I give unto you power (Authority) to tread on serpents and scorpions, and over all the power of the enemy: and nothing shall by any means hurt you.

Romans 5:17 For if by one man's offence death reigned by one; much more they which receive abundance of grace and of the gift of righteousness shall reign in life by one, Jesus Christ.)

Amplified Bible Classic (AMPC) For if because of one

man's trespass (lapse, offense) death reigned through that one, much more surely will those who receive [God's] overflowing grace (unmerited favor) and the free gift of righteousness [putting them into right standing with Himself] <u>reign as kings in life</u> through the one Man Jesus Christ (the Messiah, the Anointed One).

It is time to shout it out loud! Believers are to reign in life through our Lord Jesus Christ. We are to reign now. This passage is not talking about the past or the future but about now on planet earth.

1 John 3:2 Beloved, <u>now are we the sons of God,</u> and it doth not yet appear what we shall be: but we know that, when he shall appear, we shall be like him; for we shall see him as he is.

We are sons and daughters of the living God! And we are born to REIGN.

Revelation 1:5 And from Jesus Christ, who is the faithful witness, and the first begotten of the dead, and the prince of the kings of the earth. Unto him that loved us, and washed us from our sins in his own blood,
6 <u>And hath made us kings and priests unto God</u> and his Father; to him be glory and dominion for ever and ever. Amen.

Believers are both redeemed and restored back to dominion through the sacrificial death of our savior and Lord, Jesus Christ.

THE HALL OF FAITH

The subject of faith continues to be one of the most compelling and most intriguing of all in the Holy Scrip- tures.

The book of Hebrews, Chapter 11, is popularly known as the "Hall of Faith." It provides us with an opportuni- ty to relive and somehow experience the transforming power of a life of faith; we are ushered into a realm where all things are possible (Luke 1:37).

Firstly, my prayer to all the readers of this book is that your life will be meaningful and productive. The faith of God always produces a visible result; faith is known to give birth to miracles. May your faith produce excellent and enviable results and, may you obtain a GOOD REPORT.

For by it (faith) the elders obtained a good report (Hebrews 11:2).

Without any doubt faith ushers one to a platform where impossibility is non-existing and all things are made possible. Everything becomes doable (Mark 9:23).

GOD

Amazingly, verse 3 reveals to us that the Omnipotent employs this wonder-working principle in creation.

Through faith, we understand that the worlds were framed by the word of God, so that things which are seen were not made of things which do appear (Hebrews 11:3).

The first exercise of faith and a demonstration of its capability in this hall of faith was credited to the God of the universe in creativity as recorded in Genesis.

We see God putting His word to use in framing the worlds.

Genesis 1:1 In the beginning God created the heaven and the earth.
2   And the earth was without form, and void; and darkness was upon the face of the deep. And the Spirit of God moved upon the face of the waters.
3   And God said, Let there be light: and there was light.

Notice the first verse says God created. God's word has creative ability. So what did God do with His word? How did He bring about the creation? Notice again the involvement of the Spirit of God and how the Spirit moved upon the deep in verse two, but verse three says God spoke out what He wanted. He framed the worlds by saying what he desired and not what was prevalent.
The same verse three says, *and there was light.* Faith has produced the desired result. God just exercised dominion over the earth.

Looking again at creation from the writer of Hebrews;

so that things which are seen were not made of things which do appear (Hebrews 11:3).

The writer here makes the point that the visible creation such as the sun, stars, moon, etc., were not molded out of visible pre-existing materials, but were brought to be through the vehicle of faith.
There was no chance creation of life, no development up from some species to another by evolutionary processes.
The creation was supernaturally induced, and It came by God's power through faith.

Note that believers have unimaginable potentials regardless of where they hail from or where they find themselves.
The inference is that our faith is not to be based on what is visible or currently appears, by which we could reason out what would be, but that it is possible to emulate the God of all flesh and these heroes of faith who brought something out of that which is not through the exercise of their faith.
God made man in His image, after His likeness (exact duplication and kind) and gave Man dominion (Genesis 1:26).
The same way the Omnipotent exercised dominion as seen above is how man is expected to operate and subdue the earth.

God gave us His word as promises and believers must know that it is our heritage to utilize God's word in framing our world.

2 Peter 1:3 According as his divine power hath given unto us all things that pertain unto life and godliness, through the knowledge of him that hath called us to glory and virtue:
4 Whereby are <u>given unto us exceeding great and precious promises</u>: that by these ye might be partakers of the divine nature, having escaped the corruption that is in the world through lust.

God's word is forever settled in heaven, but we need to put it into action. It is through these promises we partake of the divine nature.

2 Corinthians 1:20 For all the promises of God in him are yea, and in him Amen, unto the glory of God by us.

Notice God's great and precious promises are given to believers to embrace as authority over every circumstance of our life.
God's word in our mouth and in our heart is how we release the creative ability of the word. We are sons and daughters of the living God. Whatever God says we can do, we can and should do the same.

May God bring something new, something glorious and something enviable out of that which is not, in your story as you continue to read this book.

ABEL

By faith Abel offered unto God a more excellent sacrifice than Cain (Hebrews 11:4).

Many Bible teachers have speculated on different reasons why one offering was accepted while the other was not. Some have said Abel offered a blood sacrifice while Cain did not, hence the rejection of Cain's sacrifice.
The scripture makes clear that Abel was a keeper of sheep while Cain was a tiller of the ground.

And she again bare his brother Abel. And Abel was a keeper of sheep, but Cain was a tiller of the ground (Genesis 4:2).

It seems they both naturally selected from that which they had reared with their own hands; which they regarded as most valuable.

The writer here helps us in retrospect to consider the occurrence through another window of perception by revealing the driving force behind Abel's offering.

By faith Abel offered unto God a more excellent sacrifice than Cain (Hebrews 11:4).

Genesis 4:4-5 gives the account of the offering made by Abel, there is no mention of 'faith,' as is true also indeed of most of the instances referred to by the apostle here. However, the book of Hebrew helps us to understand more what took place in these stories.

It's very interesting how Good News Translation (GNT) depicts Hebrew 11:4.

It was faith that made Abel offer to God a better sacrifice than Cain's. Through his faith he won God's approval as a righteous man Hebrews 11:4 (GNT)

Faith certainly made a difference. Faith apparently can make us do things that others would not dare to do. Faith DRIVES GIVING and wins God's approval.

Have you wondered why some people in Church resisted or argue about giving? Faith in God's provision seems to be the core issue.

Faith often produces or inspires a WINNING ACTION in every situation or under any dire circumstance. May your faith find that winning action in Jesus name. Summarily, faith made Abel to bring a better sacrifice to God and won His approval.

ENOCH

Let us consider the next among the heroes in this chapter;

By faith Enoch was translated that he should not see death; and was not found, because God had translated him: for before his translation he had this testimony, that he pleased God (Hebrews 11:5).

This narrative is found in Genesis 5:21-24;

Genesis 5:24 *...and Enoch walked with God:and he was not; for God took him*

Here the scripture explains that Enoch did not die and that God took him to a state of blessedness without obliging him to pass through death. The deduction here was that this holy translation is the result of his lifestyle

of faith.
Interestingly, we are told here that faith can undoubtedly defile natural laws and norms.

Faith can make one escape what others go through.

We can deduce what Enoch did. He walked with God; he simply obeyed and pleased God because of his faith.

NOAH

Another hero of faith is Noah.

By faith Noah, being warned of God of things not seen as yet, moved with fear, prepared an ark to the saving of his house; by the which he condemned the world, and became heir of the righteousness which is by faith (Hebrew 11:7).

Noah was known to be a righteous man. He was blameless among the people of his time. This does not mean Noah was perfect or sinless, but that he loved God with his whole heart and was committed to obeying God.

It is not difficult to see that Noah was influenced by faith.

And God said unto Noah, The end of all fiesh is come before me; for the earth is filled with violence through them; and, behold, I will destroy them with the earth. Make thee an ark of gopher wood; rooms shalt thou make in the ark, (Genesis 6:13-14).

By faith Noah, being warned of God of things not seen as yet, moved with fear, prepared an ark to the saving of his house; (Hebrew 11:7).

The first thing that stands out in Noah's story is the fact that he heard from God and obeyed. Noah simply obeyed God. Without seeing any sign or action, no physical evidence that what God said would come to pass, yet we have recorded in the scriptures;

Thus did Noah; according to all that God command-ed him, so did he (Genesis 6:22).

Also, we must recognize that when we walk with God, we may not have all the answers. Nothing in our present environment may make sense, yet we must be committed to obeying God's word regardless of the circumstances we find ourselves knowing whom we have believed and that at the end, we shall be vindicated.

And ultimately our action of faith and obedience will secure and deliver to us a sure reward; *and became heir of the righteousness which is by faith. Hebrew 11:7*

So faith enables creativity (Heb 11:3), faith provokes excellent sacrifices (Heb 11:4), faith pleases God (Heb 11:5-6), faith commands obedience (Heb 11:7-8).

An incontestable fact in the stories of these heroes of faith is the repeated pattern of a life of obedience to the leading of God. Noah obeyed God. Enoch obeyed God, and we see Abraham patently obeying in the following;

Hebrews 11:8 By faith Abraham, when he was called

to go out into a place which he should after receive for an inheritance, obeyed; and he went out, not knowing whither he went.

A relationship with the father will guarantee a life of obedience to everything God has said and whatever God is revealing to us. Once again, one may say, when God speaks to me I will surely obey, however, if we do not know how to obey what God has already said in His

Holy Word, one may not know how to obey the voice of the Holy Spirit.

THE DYNAMICS OF FAITH

My goal here is to discuss some of the critical elements that will undeniably influence the outcome of your faith. Knowing that it is through faith that we can access all God has done for us, we must then learn how to do this efficiently.

I aim to answer questions like:

What are these forces that will affect the result of my faith?

And how could they enable me to exercise my faith more proficiently?

My first point here is to encourage believers to have the very faith of God.

Have The God Kind Of Faith.

Believers must know that for our faith to be effective, we must have the same faith as God our father.

Mark 11:22 And Jesus answering saith unto them, <u>*Have faith in God*</u>

Note that the strength of this statement is better revealed in other translation;

Young's Literal Translation (YLT) says "*And Jesus answering saith to them, Have faith of God;*"

Or we could say that Jesus said, "Have the faith of God."

The Greek scholars inform that this same passage should be translated as, "Have the God kind of faith."

Having the God kind of faith implies a greater responsibility and demands a deeper understanding of the one exercising their faith. With the God kind of faith, you will know that your faith will work.

Let us consider the context of this critical text of the scripture. The statement was Jesus' response to Peter. He was startled, on the occasion of the fig tree (now dried up) which Jesus cursed the previous day; he called to remembrance what was done to this tree (Mark 11:12-14 and 20-21) and alerted the Lord to look at the resultant effect of his word.

Jesus then answered and said; *"Have the God kind of faith" (Mark 11:22).*

So the Lord here seized upon this moment of wonder, the disciples were in awe of what they just witnessed, and he impressed upon them the life-changing lesson of the "God kind of faith."
Having said this, he proceeded to show how this faith (God kind) works;

Mark 11:23 For verily I say unto you, That whosoever shall say unto this mountain, Be thou removed, and be thou cast into the sea; and shall not doubt in his heart, but shall believe that those things which he saith shall come to pass; he shall have whatsoever he

To make our faith work, believers are to imitate God our father as He did in Genesis 1:1-3 and also affirmed in Hebrews 11:3. The same kind of faith God used to frame our worlds is the same Jesus used, and it's the same he taught us to use in Mark 11:23.

God was not employing **'Trial And Error'** to see what may or may not work.

The God kind of faith knows there will be a success like Jesus knew his faith would work in the case of the fig tree.

In Mark 11:23 above, this faith simply operates by speaking to mountains or challenges of life and believing what you say shall be done. This is an important part of how to exercise faith victoriously. God speaks to mountains, believes His word will come to pass, and they do. Created in the image and after the likeness of God (Genesis 1:26); God designed mankind to govern the earth in the same way He rules through faith in His word. To walk in victorious and living faith, you must imitate God our father, i.e., have the faith of God or have the God-kind of faith.

Some may say, I am skeptical, and this is too much to ask. How do I operate the God kind of faith?

Ephesians 6:13 *Wherefore take unto you <u>the whole armour of God</u>, that ye may be able to withstand in the evil day, and having done all, to stand.*

Paul, some say, used this metaphor 'Armor of God' to refer to a physical armor worn by God in metaphorical battles, and that is fantastic as it helps the believer to picture or imagine it. Others say, it simply implies vigilant righteousness in general as bestowed by the grace of God, that is equally great. The bottom line is that we have an understanding of what is being described.

Think about this WHOLE ARMOR OF GOD; It is not the armor of any other being but that of God. This is what God puts on when He goes to battle, and He never lost. I say if we can wear God's armor to battle, we can certainly have the faith of God or have the God-kind of faith.

Someone may ask, how do I get this kind of faith?

You already have it if you are a believer. You only need to know how to develop it and how to release it (See Growing In Faith).

Romans 2:3 For I say, through the grace given unto me, to every man that is among you, not to think of himself more highly than he ought to think; but to think soberly, according as God hath dealt to every man the measure of faith.

God imparted faith to the unsaved for the first time when they heard the word of faith;

Romans 10:17 says, "So then faith cometh by hearing, and hearing by the word of God."

A primary barrier in the school of faith among Christians is the concept that we have to acquire more faith. The

good news is that every born-again believer already has the measure of faith (*For I say, through the grace given unto me, to every man that is among you,*).
The only challenge is, are we developing and releasing our faith? Are we growing in faith? Are we using our faith?

Ephesians 2:8 For by grace are ye saved through faith; and that not of yourselves: it is the gift of God.

Notice that both grace and faith are given to us but we must first release our faith into God's grace of salvation to be born again in the first place.

Know That God's Word Allows You To Live In Dominion

Christians should know that God's word in our heart and declared in our mouth is the way we exercise dominion upon the earth. Believers must recognize that the faith of God employs God's word to effect desired changes. Hence, the need for us to believe on the word of God with all our heart.

A key ingredient of faith is that one must believe God's word with the heart;

Romans 10:10 For with the heart man believeth unto righteousness; and with the mouth confession is made unto salvation.

For believers, we do not question the authority of God's word. After many of the disciples left following Jesus because the teaching became too hard for them, he asked the twelve, will you also go away?

John 6:68 Then Simon Peter answered him, Lord, to whom shall we go? thou hast the words of eternal life.

Christians must settle this in their heart that God's word is the word of life.
Once we have agreed on this, it becomes easier for us to accept and equally believe what God has said.

Regardless of the fact that the message did not appeal to the physical senses, Mary responded most profoundly to the word of God through angel Gabriel whom God sent to her;

Luke 1:38 And Mary said, Behold the handmaid of the Lord; <u>be it unto me according to thy word</u>. And the angel departed from her.

She accepted or submitted herself to the authority of the word of God. When God's word is believed and declared or professed, we line up ourselves for a supernatural result.

While many believers accept that God gave us dominion on earth as recorded in Genesis 1 and other passages of the Holy Scripture, some still argue that Adam lost dominion for ever to Satan.
However, whatever authority the first Adam lost, the last Adam regained for mankind.
Hence we must know that the purpose of God's heart regarding the dominion of man has not changed. Believers are to reign on earth through Jesus Christ (Romans

5:17).

The way God designed for man to reign on earth and exercise dominion is through faith-filled word of God. However, we struggle to recognize how we are to exercise the dominion.

God's way of exercising dominion is by calling things that are not as though they were until they are.

So He exercises dominion by the word of His mouth.

Rom 4:17 (As it is written, I have made thee a father of many nations,) before him whom he believed, even God, who quickeneth the dead, and <u>calleth those things which be not as though they were.</u>

This passage above teaches us how God works. God called Abraham the father of many nations when he was not in fact as if he was.

I have made thee a father of many nations. It is already a done deal. A foregone conclusion!

Theologians agree that the phrase "calling things that are not as though they were" alludes to the creation of all things out of what was not.

One can easily conclude or deduce, based on the message being passed across to us in Romans 4:17;

Rom 4:17 (As it is written, I have made thee a father of many nations,) before him whom he believed, even

*God, who quickeneth the dead, **BY** calling those things which be not as though they were.*

This is how God works. He quickens or makes alive the dead by saying what He desires. We Christians must ally ourselves to work in the same manner. We have been given dominion on earth and to exercise the dominion, we must operate as our father.

Believers are to imitate God in all we do, saying what God has said;

Ephesians 5:1 Be ye therefore followers of God, as dear children;

New Living Translation (NLT) Imitate God, therefore, in everything you do, because you are his dear children.

Jesus himself spoke what God gave him to speak;

John 12:49 For I have not spoken of myself; but the Father which sent me, he gave me a commandment, what I should say, and what I should speak.
50 And I know that his commandment is life ever-lasting: whatsoever I speak therefore, even as the Father said unto me, so I speak.

John 3:34 For he whom God hath sent speaketh the words of God: for God giveth not the Spirit by measure unto him.

Words remain the most important THINGS on planet earth. Words were the instruments by which God created all things.

Hebrews 11:3 Through faith we understand that the worlds were framed by the Word of God.
God's word is referred to as the "the word of God's power". God's word is powerful.

Hebrews 4:12 For the word of God is quick, and powerful, and sharper than any twoedged sword, piercing even to the dividing asunder of soul and spirit, and of the joints and marrow, and is a discerner of the thoughts and intents of the heart.

Luke 4:32 And they were astonished at his doctrine: for his word was with power.

Jeremiah 23:29 Is not my word like as a fire? saith the Lord; and like a hammer that breaketh the rock in pieces?

Jesus spoke faith-filled words to the fig tree, and it dried up (Mark 11:12-14). The wind and the sea obeyed his words (Mark 11:41).

Psalms 33:9 For he spake, and it was done; he commanded, and it stood fast.

God's word, when spoken by His Children in faith is a command that must be obeyed by the earth.

Hebrews 1:3 Who being the brightness of his glory, and the express image of his person, and upholding all things by the word of his power, when he had by himself purged our sins, sat down on the right hand of the Majesty on high:

Notice that God's word is the source and sustainer of all things.

God's Word Forces A Change

Isaiah revealed an ancient secret of God's word. God's word has the ability to command a change. His word can force a change when applied in faith.

*Isaiah 55:10 For <u>as the rain</u> cometh down, and the snow from heaven, and returneth not thither, but <u>watereth the earth, and maketh it</u> (**forces the earth to**) <u>bring forth</u> and bud, that it may give seed to the sower, and bread to the eater:*

*11 **<u>So shall my word be</u>** that goeth forth out of my mouth: it shall not return unto me void, but it shall accomplish that which I please, and it shall prosper in the thing whereto I sent it.*

The word of God spoken in faith, **FORCES** A CHANGE to occur on earth in our favor just as the rain waters the earth and **MAKES** it bring forth and bud in favor of the sower.

The centurion knew this secret;

Mathew 8:5 And when Jesus was entered into Capernaum, there came unto him a centurion, beseeching him,

6   And saying, Lord, my servant lieth at home sick ofthe palsy, grievously tormented.
7   And Jesus saith unto him, I will come and heal him. 8 The centurion answered and said, Lord, I am not worthy that thou shouldest come under my roof: but speak the word only, and my servant shall be healed. 9 For I am a man under authority, having soldiers under me: and I say to this man, Go, and he goeth; and to another, Come, and he cometh; and to my servant, Do this, and he doeth it.

Notice what he said; *"but speak the word only, and my servant shall be healed."*

This man knows what it means to issue a command in the military and particularly the authority of Jesus' word over every other situation including sickness.

He explains the rationale behind his understanding. As a soldier, I say to this man, go, and he goes. There is no challenge whatsoever to his authority.

Hence, God's word has unlimited authority to command a change over undesirable circumstances we may find ourselves.

Mat 8:10 When Jesus heard it, he marvelled, and said to them that followed, Verily I say unto you, I have not found so great faith, no, not in Israel.
11 And I say unto you, That many shall come from the east and west, and shall sit down with Abraham, and Isaac, and Jacob, in the kingdom of heaven.
12 But the children of the kingdom shall be cast out into outer darkness: there shall be weeping and gnashing of teeth.

13 And Jesus said unto the centurion, Go thy way; and as thou hast believed, so be it done unto thee. And his servant was healed in the selfsame hour.

It is critical for believers to recognize that God expects Man to exercise dominion through His word. There is no need to start begging for Jesus to come down from heaven to come and do something about our situations when we do have His word.

Romans 10:6 But the righteousness which is of faith speaketh on this wise, Say not in thine heart, Who shall ascend into heaven? (that is, to bring Christ down from above:)
7 Or, Who shall descend into the deep? (that is, to bring up Christ again from the dead.)

8 But what saith it? <u>The word is nigh thee, even in thy mouth, and in thy heart</u>: that is, the word of faith, which we preach;

Notice that our focus should not be on bringing Christ down from above to assist us with our troubles, but we utilize the word of faith, the Holy word of the living God by speaking it in our mouth so it can get into our heart where faith is then birthed.

2 Peter 1:19 We have also a more sure word of prophecy; whereunto ye do well that ye take heed, as unto a light that shineth in a dark place, until the day dawn, and the day star arise in your hearts:

Know That You Can Have What You Say

Some have asked, you mean I can have anything? As long as it is based on the word of God, Yes! It does not mean you run around claiming what is not included in "God's Redemptive Plan" for man.

Mark 11:23 For verily I say unto you, That whosoever shall say unto this mountain, Be thou removed, and be thou cast into the sea; and shall not doubt in his heart, <u>but shall believe that those things which he saith shall come to pass; he shall have whatsoever he saith.</u>

God laid great emphasis on what his people say. He would not have us speak haphazardly. To God, words matter. Words can build and can also break. Words can heal but can also hurt. Words have delivered and words have damaged.

God wants us to learn to speak right and with purpose. Words cannot be spoken aimlessly, carelessly or casually. God would have you respect your tongue.

Words, as said earlier, remain the most important THINGS on planet earth.

Mathew 6:31 <u>Therefore take no thought, saying, What shall we eat? or, What shall we drink? or, Wherewithal shall we be clothed?</u>
32 (For after all these things do the Gentiles seek:) for your heavenly Father knoweth that ye have need of all these things.

Jesus taught the lesson of taking any thought that filters through our mind (_take no thought, saying,_) AND SPEAKING THEM. Some thoughts, we are to reject steadfastly and cast away rather than embrace or release them through our mouth. They can be costly. Saying these words will give life to them.

Jesus said what you keep putting in your mind will ultimately come out of your mouth. He also said you would account for your words on the day of judgment. And he gave advice on how words do deliver and how words can condemn.

Mathew 12:36 But I say unto you, That every idle word that men shall speak, they shall give account thereof in the day of judgment.
37 For by thy words thou shalt be justified, and by thy words thou shalt be condemned.

In the light of the preceding, God corrected Jeremiah who was afraid to say what God tells him to go and say;

Jeremiah 1:7 Then said I, Ah, Lord God! behold, I cannot speak: for I am a child.
7 But the Lord said unto me, Say not, I am a child: for thou shalt go to all that I shall send thee, and whatsoever I command thee thou shalt speak.

God said to him; do not verbalize your weakness. '*Say not, I am a child,*' but whatever I say to you, go and say the same.
Saying what is, will continue to give us more of

what is. Saying what God said or saying our desire, according to the word of God, is the way to change our unwanted circumstances.
Believers should know that professing our weakness will not profit us anyhow;

Joel 3:10 Beat your plowshares into swords and your pruninghooks into spears: <u>let the weak say, I am strong.</u>

God will have us declare what He has said in his word until the word grows and prevails and become the situation of our life (Acts 19:20);

Psalms 91:1 He that dwelleth in the secret place of the most High shall abide under the shadow of the Almighty.
2 <u>I will say of the Lord, He is my refuge and my fortress:</u> my God; in him will I trust.

Psalms 107:2 <u>Let the redeemed of the Lord say so,</u> whom he hath redeemed from the hand of the enemy;

Hebrew 13:5 Let your conversation be without covetousness; and be content with such things as ye have: for he hath said, I will never leave thee, nor forsake thee.
6 <u>So that we may boldly say,</u> The Lord is my helper, and I will not fear what man shall do unto me.

Saying what God has said is our way to victory in life.

God will not have us murmur and complain. We must

learn to respond to our thoughts, circumstances, and temptations in faith using the word of God as Christ did.

Proverbs 18:21 Death and life are in the power of the tongue: and they that love it shall eat the fruit thereof.

Proverbs 5:6 Suffer not thy mouth to cause thy fiesh to sin; neither say thou before the angel, that it was an error: wherefore should God be angry at thy voice, and destroy the work of thine hands?

See how our speech can provoke what is not desired, learn to speak well.

Numbers 14:27 How long shall I bear with this evil congregation, which murmur against me? I have heard the murmurings of the children of Israel, which they murmur against me.
28 Say unto them, As truly as I live, saith the Lord, as ye have spoken in mine ears, so will I do to you:

God is listening in when we speak; '*as you have spoken in mine ears,*' mind your language, therefore.
God is activated by words. Angels are activated by words. So also evil powers are activated by words.

Apostle James helped to unravel the need to bridle the tongue;

James 1:26 If any man among you seem to be religious, and bridleth not his tongue, but deceiveth his own heart, this man's religion is vain.

James 3:4 Behold also the ships, which though they be so great, and are driven of fierce winds, yet are they turned about with a very small helm, whithersoever the governor listeth.
5 Even so the tongue is a little member, and boasteth great things. Behold, how great a matter a little fire kindleth!

The Apostle compared the tongue of man to the little helm of a ship that controls the entire direction of the whole ship. The tongue is equally a little member of the body and yet pilots or determine the direction of the life of an individual. This little but powerful member must be brought under control by the help of the Spirit of God. The power of life and death lie in it as we know.

Proverbs 13:3 He that keepeth his mouth keepeth his life: but he that openeth wide his lips shall have destruction.

When God wanted to create the world, He spoke. Words have creative power. Your tongue is one of the greatest gifts you are endowed with by the heavenly father. Learn to use it appropriately.

Jesus said what you say, can defile;

Mathew 15:17-20 Do not ye yet understand, that whatsoever entereth in at the mouth goeth into the belly, and is cast out into the draught?
18 But those things which proceed out of the mouth come forth from the heart; and they defile the man.

Jesus taught us to address life mountains by speaking to them Mark 11:23.
Complaints and murmuring cannot help. Telling others about them is not the same as speaking to them.

Remember that saying what is, establishes the present.

God never validated darkness or discuss it although it was there in Genesis. He called out what he wanted. Genesis 1:3 Let there be light, and there was light. God's way of doing things is calling things that be not as though they were Romans 4:17

Our tongues have the ability to activate the angelic ministry;
Hebrews 1:14 Are they not all ministering spirits, sent forth to minister for them who shall be heirs of salvation?

How do they do this?

Ps 103:20 Bless the Lord, ye his angels, that excel in strength, that do his commandments, <u>hearkening unto the voice of his word.</u>

Angels watch out for God's word. Their ministry is activated by the sound of God's word.

Know That Living Faith Has Corresponding Action

One of the most distorted aspects of faith in the Church and yet, much simplified in the Bible is the subject of 'Faith And Corresponding Action.'

The Bible makes clear that your ACTION is what shows that your faith is ALIVE. Your actions or works have to correspond with what you are believing for if you are to receive from God.

Many unfortunately try to draw a parallel between the works produced by faith and the works of the law. These two are not the same. Paul and James did not contradict themselves as many alleged.

Romans 3:28 Therefore we conclude that a man is justified by faith <u>without the deeds of the law.</u> (at salvation).

James 2:24 Ye see then how that by works (that correspond to our faith after salvation) a man is justified, and not by faith only.

There are no contradictions in these statements <u>if we look at the targets of these texts in the passages.</u>

Paul in the book of Romans is focused on how to become a Christian, he targeted the beginning of relationship with God and emphasized the absence of the works of the law that compete or contend with faith;

Ephesians 2:8 For by grace are ye saved through faith; and that not of yourselves: it is the gift of God:
9 Not of works, lest any man should boast.

James, however, is focused on what it means to live as a Christian. Christians should be Christianly; my Christianity should affect my fellow human being. He emphasized works that complete our faith produced as fruits of God's Spirit on the inside of us;

James 2:15 If a brother or sister be naked, and destitute of daily food,
16 And one of you say unto them, Depart in peace, be ye warmed and filled; notwithstanding ye give them not those things which are needful to the body; what doth it profit?
17 Even so faith, if it hath not works, is dead, being alone.

Paul affirmed the same that the faith of a Christian produces corresponding actions;

Ephesians 2:10 For we are his workmanship, <u>created in Christ Jesus unto good works</u>, which God hath before ordained that we should walk in them.

1 Thessalonians 1:3 Remembering without ceasing <u>your work of faith,</u> and labour of love, and patience of hope in our Lord Jesus Christ, in the sight of God and our Father

New International Version (NIV)
We remember before our God and Father <u>your work</u>

So we are not saved by our works, but we are saved to
work. The Spirit of God in us must bear fruits that are
visible.
There is the gift of righteousness imputed to Man at
salvation, and there is the work of righteousness now
produced because of this imputed righteousness through
the inner working of the Holy Spirit.

*Galatians 5:22 But the fruit of the Spirit is love, joy,
peace, longsuffering, gentleness, goodness, faith,*

Faith's corresponding action is all about DOING what
we learn or see God doing in His word and DOING what
corresponds with trust and confidence that what we
believed God for IS ALREADY DONE.

Christians should study the scriptures and as we do, we
know more of God's character. And as we discover more
about Him, we emulate Him by acting out His word in
whatsoever situation we find ourselves as James discussed
above. God's word is to be acted upon.

Mathew 7:24 Therefore whosoever heareth these

sayings of mine, and doeth them, I will liken him unto a wise man, which built his house upon a rock:
25   And the rain descended, and the fioods came, and the winds blew, and beat upon that house; and it fellnot: for it was founded upon a rock.

26   And every one that heareth these sayings of mine, and doeth them not, shall be likened unto a foolish man, which built his house upon the sand:
27   And the rain descended, and the fioods came, and the winds blew, and beat upon that house; and it fell:and great was the fall of it.

James 1:22 But be ye doers of the word, and not hearers only, deceiving your own selves.
23 For if any be a hearer of the word, and not a doer, he is like unto a man beholding his natural face in a glass:

24 For he beholdeth himself, and goeth his way, and straightway forgetteth what manner of man he was.
25 But whoso looketh into the perfect law of liberty, and continueth therein, he being not a forgetful hearer, but a doer of the work, this man shall be blessed in his deed.

James 2:18 Yea, a man may say, Thou hast faith, and I have works: shew me thy faith without thy works, and <u>I will shew thee my faith by my works.</u>

Your corresponding action of faith announces your faith!

Mark 2.1 And again he entered into Capernaum after some days; and it was noised that he was in the house. 2 And straightway many were gathered together, insomuch that there was no room to receive them, no, not so much as about the door: and he preached the word unto them. 3 And they come unto him, bringing one sick of the palsy, which was borne of four. 4 And when they could not come nigh unto him for the press, they uncovered the roof where he was: and when they had broken it up, they let down the bed wherein the sick of the palsy lay. 5 <u>When Jesus saw their faith</u>, he said unto the sick of the palsy, Son, thy sins be forgiven thee.

Notice that in agreement with James *("I will shew thee my faith by my works")*, the Lord Jesus saw the faith of the team bringing the man sick of the palsy. You cannot see faith as it were, but you can certainly see the actions of faith.

James 2:26 For as the body without the spirit is dead, so faith without works is dead also. (James said DOING nothing kills faith).

The heroes of faith as recorded in Hebrews 11 all have corresponding actions to their faith;

God SPOKE His desire into the darkness that existed Hebrews 11:3.

Abel GAVE a more excellent sacrifice than Cain Hebrews 11:4.

Enoch before God took him, PLEASED God Hebrews 11:5.

Noah moved to OBEY what God told him regarding the Ark Hebrews 11:7.

Abraham fully OBEYED God's call to leave his country Hebrews 11:8.

GROWING IN FAITH

2 Thess 1:3 We are bound to thank God always for you, brethren, as it is meet, <u>because that your faith groweth exceedingly, and the charity of every one of you all toward each other aboundeth;</u>
Notice above that a changed character and better attitude in believers is predicated upon their faith growing ex- ceedingly. So faith impacts our attitude.

Learn To Feed Your Spirit

While the scripture informs that God gave to every believer the measure of faith (Romans 12:3), for your faith to grow, believers must learn to feed the word of God into their heart. It is very crucial for us to understand that the heart or the spirit of man plays a very important role in our faith walk. Strong and enduring faith is built upon the foundation of a persuaded heart.

Romans 10:10 For <u>with the heart man believeth</u> unto righteousness;

Proverbs 7:1 My son, <u>keep my words</u>, and lay up my commandments with thee.
2 Keep my commandments, and live; and my law as the apple of thine eye.
3 Bind them upon thy fingers, <u>write them upon the table of thine heart.</u>

Notice in the above passages that the heart is a critical bedrock of a successful faith life. It takes the heart of man to believe God's word, and the word can only be believed when it is fed to the heart or spirit of man. We, therefore, need to continue to deliberately improve the heart condition by feeding it with the word of life.

Hear God's word and His promises at every opportunity. In your car, when you are about to sleep, or when cooking or eating in the kitchen, etc., feed the heart.

Mathew 4:4 But he answered and said, It is written, Man shall not live by bread alone, but by every word that proceedeth out of the mouth of God.

Know that as bread is to the body for STRENGTH, even so, is the word of God to the spirit of man for FAITH. For faith to come alive and stay alive, it must be fed, just as any living organism needs feeding for sustenance.

Romans 10:17 So then faith cometh by hearing, and hearing by the word of God.

God's word imparts supernatural faith into the heart of the hearer.
This faith is not the same as common human faith inherent in all men. This can only believe what it can feel, see, taste, hear, or smell. It is why many of us can sit in a chair we've never sat in and believe it will hold us up. We fly in airplanes when we don't fully understand how they work, and we don't know the pilot, but we believe all will be well.
But there is a supernatural faith of God that is only

imparted by hearing God's word. God's word is called the word of faith (Rom 10:8).
Faith can come alive strongly when the heart is well fed, while faith can also leave when the heart is starved of the necessary word of God.

The body of Christ should note that the presence of fear is an indication that the spirit of man needs to be fed the necessary food. It was David who said; *What time I am afraid, I will trust in thee* (Psalms 56:3).
The way God built Man is that our faith rises or fall by what we allow into the heart. We can hear the news that will command fear and open us up to attack while we can also hear words that will build our confidence and faith up and assure us of victory.

This is why God commands us;

Proverbs 4.23 Keep thy heart with all diligence; for out of it are the issues of life.

Philippians 4:8 Finally, brethren, whatsoever things are true, whatsoever things are honest, whatsoever things are just, whatsoever things are pure, whatsoever things are lovely, whatsoever things are of good report; if there be any virtue, and if there be any praise, think on these things.

1 Timothy 4:15 Meditate upon these things; give thyself wholly to them; that thy profiting may appear to all.

Proverbs 4:20 My son, attend to my words; incline thine ear unto my sayings.

21 Let them not depart from thine eyes; <u>keep them in the midst of thine heart.</u>

All these scriptures and more reveal that you can gain control of your own thought life, you should not allow the enemy to determine what you hear, think or imagine, you have a say in it.
You can choose to keep your heart with great diligence, choose to think on what is true, choose to meditate on God's word and choose to give attention to God's word.

God's word is food for our spirits. As food is strength or life to the flesh, God's word is the life source of the spirit of man.

Jn 6:63 It is the spirit that quickeneth; the fiesh profiteth nothing: the words that I speak unto you, they are spirit, and they are life.

God's word is for our spirit, Jesus said. The believer should endeavor to keep them; *<u>keep them in the midst of thine heart,</u>* (Proverbs 4:20).

Romans 10:17 So then faith cometh by hearing, and hearing by the word of God.

Learn To Release Or Use Your Faith.

Faith is released by speaking it.

Rom 4:17 (As it is written, I have made thee a father of many nations,) before him whom he believed, even God, who quickeneth the dead, and calleth those things which be not as though they were.

Here we have God's MO (modus operandi) declared. This is God's way of doing things; He quickens the dead or raises the dead by calling those things which are not as though they were. Our God turns things around by saying what He wants.

Faith is released by your words. Paul referred to David in Psalms 116 that when you believe, you should speak. It is how faith is meant to work. Your faith is revealed by what you say. Nothing changes physically until we say what we believe.

Your faith can change your world! But no matter how great your faith is you must first release your faith if it is going to change the circumstances that are affecting you negatively.

2 Corinthians 4:13 We having <u>the same spirit of faith, according as it is written, I believed, and therefore have I spoken</u>; we also believe, and therefore speak;

Genesis 1:3 And God said, Let there be light: and there was light.

Your faith will not rise beyond your confession. The Apostles came to Jesus and asked for him to increase their faith;

Luke 17:5 And the apostles said unto the Lord, Increase our faith.
6 And the Lord said, If ye had faith as a grain of

mustard seed, ye might say unto this sycamine tree, Be thou plucked up by the root, and be thou planted in the sea; and it should obey you.

The answer is simplistic and very clearly stated.
"If ye had faith as a grain of mustard seed, <u>ye might say</u>"
Faith works like a seed, the way you plant it is by saying it. So say or speak your faith, and the circumstance should obey you.

Romans 10:6 But the righteousness which is of faith speaketh on this wise, Say not in thine heart, Who shall ascend into heaven? (that is, to bring Christ down from above:)

7 Or, Who shall descend into the deep? (that is, to bring up Christ again from the dead.)
8 <u>But what saith it? The word is nigh thee, even in thy mouth, and in thy heart:</u> that is, the word of faith, which we preach;

Notice this same powerful principle cleverly expressed by Paul. Believers (righteousness which is of faith) don't go around crying for Jesus to come down from heaven and do something about their challenges, but what they do is make use of the promises of God by confessing and declaring the word of faith which is given to us. Believers must learn to speak the word of God to their circumstances.
Romans 10:10 For with the heart man believeth unto righteousness; <u>and with the mouth confession is made unto salvation.</u>

Consider the story beneath;

Mark 4:37 And there arose a great storm of wind, and the waves beat into the ship, so that it was now full.
38 And he was in the hinder part of the ship, asleep on a pillow: and they awake him, and say unto him, Master, carest thou not that we perish?
39 And he arose, and rebuked the wind, and said unto the sea, Peace, be still. And the wind ceased, and there was a great calm.

40 And he said unto them, Why are ye so fearful? how is it that ye have no faith?
41 And they feared exceedingly, and said one to another, What manner of man is this, that even the wind and the sea obey him?

Verse 40 showed that Jesus expected his disciples to handle the storm by their faith in his word that they should go to the other side (Mark 4:35). "*Why are ye so fearful? How is it that ye have no faith?*" So, we understand that they had fear and they had no faith. Notice the only statement recorded in verse 38 and credited to the disciples in this episode is the evidence of their fear and lack of faith; "*Master, carest thou not that we perish?*"

The status of our faith is revealed by what we say. Some may say we have faith, but their confession is inconsistent with a heart full of faith. Know that your faith will not rise beyond your confession. Therefore, learn to first feed your faith and then release it.

FAITH AND PRAYER SYNERGY

Believers should study keenly and desire the mastery of the cooperation between faith and prayer. This is un- doubtedly a notable feat for the New Testament believer.

A great Man of God once described these two tools and said, "Prayer is certainly the key, but faith opens the door." My point is there is a connection, a synergy between this two power tools and when we have a mastery of these tools and understand how they com- plement one another, we can be more effective in both our prayer and faith walk.

Faith and Prayer are power twins and Christians should endeavor to understand the unbreakable connection between these two tools given to believers.

It could be as simple as, after an intense prayer for a new job, what next? Faith is then needed to get up and approach necessary people or go to places for job op- portunities. In other words, knowing the right thing to do or the right thing to say after prayer is as critical as the prayer itself.

Notice the Lord establishing a relationship between this two in his statement to the disciples after the fig tree he spoke to withered;

Mathew 21:21 Jesus answered and said unto them,

Verily I say unto you, <u>If ye have faith, and doubt not,</u> ye shall not only do this which is done to the fig tree, but also if ye shall say unto this mountain, Be thou removed, and be thou cast into the sea; it shall be done.
22 And <u>all things, whatsoever ye shall ask in prayer, believing, ye shall receive</u>.

The first thing to note is that faith works by saying, without having to pray.

Jesus never prayed about the fig tree, he only spoke to it (Mathew 21:19 and 21).

Mark 11:13 And seeing a fig tree afar off having leaves, he came, if haply he might find any thing thereon: and when he came to it, he found nothing but leaves; for the time of figs was not yet.
14 And Jesus answered and said unto it, <u>No man eat fruit of thee hereafter for ever.</u> And his disciples heard it.

We see clearly above that no prayer was involved; only faith-filled words. So we establish that God's word works by saying it without you praying it.

The second point to note in Mathew 21:22 is that when we have prayed, we still have to keep the right faith attitude. *And <u>all things, whatsoever ye shall ask in prayer, BELIEVING, ye shall receive</u>.*

I have seen many people after praying and leaving the place of prayer; their confession was inconsistent with what they prayed about. Jesus said after prayer you need to continue or remain in faith (BELIEVING) that what you prayed for is already done and that you will soon have the answer.

When you are in faith, you must pay attention to what you THINK (what you allow in your mind), what you SAY and what you DO.

The book of James helps shed more light on this synergy between faith and prayer;

James 5:14 Is any sick among you? let him call for the elders of the church; and let them pray over him, anointing him with oil in the name of the Lord:
15 And the prayer of faith shall save the sick, and the Lord shall raise him up; and if he have committed sins, they shall be forgiven him.

James 1:5 If any of you lack wisdom, let him ask of God, that giveth to all men liberally, and upbraideth not; and it shall be given him.
6 But let him ask in faith, NOTHING WAVERING. For he that wavereth is like a wave of the sea driven with the wind and tossed.

7 For let not that man think that he shall receive any thing of the Lord.
8 A double minded man is unstable in all his ways.

The scripture makes clear again the cooperation between this great gifts of faith and prayer. Prayer, as written above, MUST be done in faith *(let him ask in faith)*.

This implies the state where the believer keeps believing in and after prayer that what they had requested shall undoubtedly be delivered to them.

Solomon after asking for wisdom was immediately presented with the opportunity to either reject or manifest this wisdom (1 Kings 3). Thank God he received and manifested it.

To waver means to be undecided, be irresolute, hesitate, vacillate, fluctuate, think twice or take a second thought, change one's mind.
Notice that once we waver in our thoughts, it will impact what we say and what we do regarding what we have prayed for.

Consider the following beneath;

Mathew 17:15 Lord, have mercy on my son: for he is lunatick, and sore vexed: for ofttimes he falleth into the fire, and oft into the water.
16 And I brought him to thy disciples, and they could not cure him.

17 Then Jesus answered and said, O faithless and perverse generation, how long shall I be with you? how long shall I suffer you? bring him hither to me.

Here again, we find cooperation between faith and prayer established by the Lord. A man brought his lunatic son to be ministered to by the disciples, but they could not cast him out.
Notice that the first thing Jesus said was responsible for

their inability to prevail was their faithlessness *(O faith-less generation)*. And again we see the disciples approaching him privately and asking for why they could not cast him out;

Mathew 17:19 Then came the disciples to Jesus apart, and said, Why could not we cast him out?
20 And Jesus said unto them, <u>Because of your unbelief</u>: for verily I say unto you, If ye have faith as a grain of mustard seed, ye shall say unto this mountain, Remove hence to yonder place; and it shall remove; and nothing shall be impossible unto you.
21 Howbeit this kind goeth not out but by prayer and fasting.

Many have hastily jumped to the conclusion that prayer and fasting alone is the key to casting out stubborn forces and thus missing out on the lesson here. Notice the Lord once again emphasizing the synergy between faith and prayer. In Mathew 17:20, he informs the disciples again that the failure was a faith failure *(Because of your unbelief)*, however, in Mathew 17:21, he delivered to us the solution to the weakness in our faith operation as prayer and fasting.

So we thus establish the synergy between faith and prayer.

Praise God!